ACIDIC PRAYER IN

WRESTLING WITH GOD IN THE MIDST OF PAIN

ISBN 978 9914 50 075 2

info@urimthummiment.com

X - @MarylineNappah

WhatsApp & Cell: +254714655357

ACIDIC PRAYER IN

WRESTLING WITH GOD IN THE MIDST OF PAIN

TABLE OF CONTENTS

So Jotham became mighty (glorious) because he prepared his ways before the Lord, his God. 2 Chro. 27:6

Under normal circumstances, nothing happens until there is an action that causes a movement in a particular direction. Things both in the spiritual and physical realms will continue to assume a position of rest until force acts on them. In the Christian faith, until you arise from your inside, your outside will not experience action that produces results and fruits. If the sun does not arise every morning, the world will remain in darkness. If a man does not arise to challenge his challenges, oppose his opposition, attack his attackers, and frustrate his frustrations, there can be no change, and his future and destiny will have nothing to show for it.

Trouble will continue to trouble you and harass you until you harass it back. Your silence is the devil's advantage. In the realm of the spirit, silence means you agree with or accept what is happening. The psalmist said, "When I kept silent, my bones wasted away…. ***Ps 32:3***". People of God, you have gone through pain, frustration, and ridicule for too long. That problem has mocked you long enough. It is time for a change; let there be a Holly

Recreation in us against it, for heavens depends on your declaration. Goliath of Gath was protected all over his body but had an unprotected forehead, and the stone went straight to the opened forehead and pulled the giant down, so also, every problem in your life has an unprotected forehead. There are spiritual bullets and stones to hit your Goliath on your unprotected forehead to bring you down.

Acts 12:10; When the church prayed, the iron gate opened for Peter. Get ready because every iron gate or barrier against your life and destiny is about to be flung open in Jesus' name.

Remember that if you don't pray, you become a prey, the distance between you and your miracle is a prayer away. So, pray until something happens, ***Matt 11:12***. And from the days of John the Baptist until now, the kingdom of heaven has suffered violence, and the violent have taken it by force. "Child of God, we live in a crooked, rowdy world full of wickedness. ***Psalm 74:20*** says, "........ For the dark places of the earth are full of the habitations of cruelty/ wickedness. Arise and do something to undo every form of wickedness the enemy has committed against your life and destiny. If you don't pray to succeed, you must pray to survive.

Get ready to enjoy an abundant life in all areas of your life.

Dear brethren,

As you read and confess these scriptures, the word of God will prevail over your circumstances, and you will enjoy an abundant life.

First, denounce the devil out of your life, e.g., marriage, finances, business, job, body, etc., and invite Jesus Christ to come and give you abundant life, even as you study and apply the following scriptures.

1. For abundant mercy: read ***Isaiah 55:7*** and ***Romans 8:1–2*** (KJV) and then apply: I....................(Put your name) repent of all my sins, known or unknown, and I ask the Lord Jesus Christ to cleanse me with his precious blood. Therefore, the Lord have mercy on me, and there is therefore no condemnation in me, for

I am in Christ Jesus, and I walk not after the flesh but after the spirit. I am free from sin and its effects, for the Lord has abundantly pardoned me in Jesus' name, Amen.

2. For abundant peace: read ***Psalms 37:11*** (KJV) and then apply: I.................................(Put your name). As I humble myself to the Lord, I will inherit the earth, and I will delight in abundant peace given through Jesus Christ and according to ***Philippians 4:7***. The peace of God, which surpasses all understanding, keeps my heart and mind through Christ Jesus. I denounce every fear in my heart and mind in Jesus' name, and I welcome the peace of God in Jesus name, Amen.

3. For abundant Grace and Supply: Read ***2Corinthians 9:8, Philippians 4:19, and Psalms 132:15***. And then apply: I...(Put your name) My god is able to make all grace abound towards me so that I will always have all sufficiency in all things and I will abound for every good work for all my needs have been supplied for and my provision is abundantly

blessed, and I am satisfied with bread in Jesus name, Amen.

4. For abundant entrance: Read ***2 Peter 1:11***. Remember that as a child of God, everything that you need is in the kingdom of God, so apply: I.........................(Put your name.) In everything that I need, even though there seems to be no way, God will make a way for me, and entrance shall be ministered unto me abundantly into the kingdom of our Lord and Savior Jesus Christ, amen.

5. For abundant power: read ***Ephesians 3:20–21,*** and then apply: I............................(Put your name) God is able to do exceedingly, abundantly above all that I ask or think according to the power that worketh in us, and I will give him glory in the church for my Christ Jesus, the world is without end, in Jesus' name, Amen.

6. For abundant riches and honor: Read ***2 Chronicles 17:5,*** and then apply: I.......................(Put your name). Just like Jehoshaphat, the Lord will establish my life in his

hand, and all nations will bring to me riches and honor in abundance, in Jesus' name, Amen.

7. Finally, back to ***John 10:10;*** An abundant life, and then apply: I......................(Put your name) Today in my marriage, finances, job, business, church, home, and body, I will enjoy an abundant life in Jesus' name, Amen, Amen, Amen.

With you in God's love.

Genesis 41: 1–44; Proverbs 4: 1–27; 1 Kings 3: 5–15; Daniel 1: 17; Daniel 2: 1–23; Ephesians 1: 7–8; Psalms 90: 12–17

Dear Lord Jesus,

Lord Most High, on this day... I choose to worship you. I say hallelujah to the most high, and I glorify your name. Breathe upon me and breathe new life into my life in every area of my life, into my heart, into my spirit, and into my mind. This day, oh Lord, I come to ask you for wisdom. Fill my mind with wisdom and my heart too.

Wisdom is all I ask for; it is the principal thing that will exalt me, the wisdom that will guide me, and the wisdom that will take me to the top. The wisdom that will make me number one. The wisdom that will keep me ahead.

I declare I will not be destroyed by foolishness, but your wisdom will arise in my life, the wisdom of the Almighty God. As I stand in Your presence today, no devil, no curse, no principality, no rulers from hell, no evil, no sorcery, no stronghold, no ruler of darkness, no powers
of hell shall stand in my promotion, in my going forward,

in my exaltation in the mighty name of our Lord Jesus Christ of Nazareth.

Today, as I stand in your authority, the authority of your Spirit, the authority of your Power, and the authority of the Blood of the lamb Jesus Christ, I bind all the powers of Hell, all the powers of darkness, that have held my life stagnant; I bind them and I render them powerless; I destroy them out of my life, out of my name, and out of my education and academics; I burn them to ashes in the mighty name of Jesus; and I bury them never to come back into my life in the powers of hell that have been pulling our lives backwards day by day, destroying the works of my hands, destroying my good performance in my academics, destroying my relationships, destroying the foundations that I have laid, destroying my businesses, you enemies of my labor, today I bind you all agents of Lucifer and I command you to get out of my name, out of my academics, out of the works of my hand, out of my life, and out of my system. I render you

powerless, and I crush your head under my feet in the mighty name of our Lord Jesus Christ, Son of the most high God. Every spirit of deceitfulness, every spirit that has been tormenting my life, every lying spirit, every spirit of confusion, every voice of Jezebel, you spirit of fear, every devil speaking to my mind I bind you today, tormenting spirits, I bind you today, I pull down your stronghold out of my mind, you spirit of fear, you spirit of reproach, you spirits of confusion, you red, white and black witchcraft, get out of my life, out of my names, I cut out your tongues, I nullify your works and operations, and I declare your purpose shall not prevail or prosper in my life, in my education, in my academics. I drive you away, and I destroy you by fire in the mighty name of our Lord Jesus Christ.

You prince of the evil, the principalities of the hierarchy of the evil, you queen of the evil, all rulers of darkness that rule upwards, Jezebel spirits, demonic spirits of poverty and destruction, I bind you today, dragons from the sea, those that rule under the earth and around the earth are bound today, your strongholds are brought down, your altars are overthrown, and you are uprooted out of my life, out of my name and out of everything called by my name, in the mighty name of Jesus Christ, you are destroyed by fire, in the mighty name of Jesus Christ of Nazareth, son of the most high God. And in the name of Jesus, I declare today that no weapon that is fashioned against me shall prosper, be it any physical or spiritual negative weapon, it shall not prosper, and from today, the word of God and his wisdom are my shield, all weapons of darkness, the Lord Jesus rebukes you, the Lord Jesus refutes you, the Lord Jesus nullifies your works in my life, and you are destroyed and uprooted by your roots out of my life in the name of Jesus Christ.

Awesome God, I pray that you may begin to lift my life, that you may begin to clothe me with the robes of honor, the robes of righteousness, the robes of glory, the robes of favor, and the robes of wisdom, that you may begin to crown my head, put a ring on my finger like you did for Joseph, begin to pull me out of my dungeons, begin to command the pharaohs of this world to move on my behalf, and let the angels of heaven begin to minister now on my behalf to the Glory and the Honor of your name.

Everything that you have prepared for me, Lord, that belongs to me at this level, I don't want to miss it, for I am a joint heir with Christ. Today I draw near to you, even expecting to receive the inheritance you have for me.

Today I take the yoke of Jesus Christ and put it on me, and I enter into rest in the name of Jesus Christ. Fill me, oh LORD, with your wisdom, which is a gift to me. I thank you, and I worship your Holy name, Amen and Amen

Phil 4:19: But my God shall supply all your needs according to His riches in glory through Christ Jesus.

1. Every day, let the pillar of fire of the living God go before me and light up my pathways in Jesus' name.
2. Holy Spirit, cleanse my heart with your fire and the blood of the Lamb in Jesus' name.
3. Holy Spirit, inflame my heart with the love of Christ in Jesus' name.
4. Oh Lord, let the fruit of the spirit begin to manifest in my life in a powerful new way in the name of Jesus.
5. Let every stronghold of idolatry in my heart be thrown down and destroyed by the thundering fire of God, in Jesus' name.
6. Oh Lord, give unto me your word of wisdom through the spirit in Jesus' name.
7. Oh Lord, give me the gift of prophecy through the spirit, in Jesus' name.
8. Oh Lord, give unto me the gift of discernment through the spirit, in Jesus' name.
9. Lord, help me to use your gifts to glorify your name and edify the body of Christ in Jesus' name.

10. Oh, spirit of life that raised Jesus from the dead, breathe life into my;

    - Prayer altar
    - dream life
    - Marriage
    - Calling
    - every organ in my body

11. Every satanic covering preventing me from seeing in the spirit, be consumed by the fire of God in Jesus' name.
12. Every strongman throwing evil spirit blanket over my eyes in the spirit, be consumed by the fire of the Lord in Jesus' name.
13. Spirit of the living God, open my eyes to see in the spirit, in Jesus' name.
14. Oh Lord, open my ears to hear your voice clearly in Jesus' name.
15. Oh, Lord, release your anointing of excellence upon my life in the name of Jesus.
16. It is written: "The Lord shall make me the head and not the tail; I shall be above and not beneath in the name of Jesus."
17. You spirit of the tail, lose your hold upon my life in the name of Jesus.
18. I refuse to sink in the sea of life, in Jesus' name.

19. I paralyze every agent of shame and reproach in the name of Jesus.
20. Any voice calling me to the tail position be silenced by the blood of Jesus.
21. Every power occupying my seat of greatness, be unseated by fire in the name of Jesus.
22. As I stamp my feet. On the ground, so shall my territory be enlarged in Jesus' name.
23. I paralyze every satanic competition for... (mention the position here) by fire in the name of Jesus.
24. Let my season of glory appear in the name of Jesus.
25. Every Goliath and pharaoh bragging and boasting against my God shall be bound and cast into the Lake of Fire in the name of Jesus.
26. Every satanic expectation against my destiny, be disappointed in the name of Jesus.
27. Let the hornets of the Lord be released against my full-time enemies in the name of Jesus.
28. I recover all that the enemy has stolen from me in the dream, in Jesus' name.
29. Every satanic chain binding my hands from prospering, catch fire and burn to ashes in Jesus' name.

30. Every satanic chain on my neck pulling me backward, catch fire and burn to ashes in Jesus' name.
31. Every satanic chain on my waist dragging me down, catch fire, and burn to ashes in Jesus' name.
32. Every satanic chain on my feet hindering me from moving forward, break and burn to ashes in Jesus' name.
33. I jump out of every circle of defeat and failure because of the power in the blood of Jesus.
34. In Jesus' name, I pray that every seed of failure in my life be consumed by the fire of God.
35. In Jesus' name, let every tree of non-achievement planted in my family line be uprooted by fire.
36. Satanic anchor on my hands and feet, be roasted in Jesus' Mighty name.
37. By the power of the blood of Jesus, I move from where I am now to where God wants me to be.
38. I break and lose myself from every curse of non-achievement in Jesus' name.
39. Every satanic initiation in the dream will be canceled and nullified by the blood of Jesus Christ.
40. I shall sing of the goodness and mercy of the Lord forever, in Jesus' name.

******* Lord, I thank you for answering my prayers

1. ***Gen 8:12;*** I declare and confess that the season of harvest will not cease in my life, in Jesus' name.
2. ***Isaiah 45:1–3;*** Every hidden treasure and abundance be exposed to me in Jesus' name.
3. ***Isaiah 60:5; 61:5-6;*** I claim all the riches of the ungodly to come into my hands in Jesus' name.
4. ***Ps 1:1-3;*** I prophesy God's increase on all that belongs to me, that it will grow exceedingly in Jesus' name.
5. ***Matt 13:24-25;*** Destroy every evil seed planted in my prosperity, in Jesus' name.
6. ***Luk 6:38;*** I will reap a bumper harvest from every seed I have sown in Jesus' name.
7. ***Num 23:23;*** I declare that every evil seed sown against my life and destiny that I do not know about will not germinate/ prosper in Jesus' name.
8. ***Mk 4:20;*** I declare that every good seed I have sown in the kingdom will attract a hundredfold harvest to me in Jesus' name.

9. ***Isaiah 49:22-23;*** Prophesy into your future that God will begin to bring you the riches of the gentiles in Jesus' name.
10. ***Isaiah 3:10;*** I take authority over every devourer, and I destroy all their efforts and effects over all my labor in Jesus' name.
11. ***Isaiah 61:9;*** Wherever I find myself in this life, the blessings of God shall be evident in my life, in Jesus' n

Ps 24:1; Ecl 5:9. The goodness and abundance of the land are not for some selected few. When God was creating the world, he had you in mind. Because of that, you will be sucking the milk and honey of this land, and no man or woman will take your portion in Jesus' name.

1. ***Isaiah 1:19; Deut 11:9;*** In Jesus' name, I will partake of the best of this land, its milk and honey.
2. ***Deut 11:11-12;*** when there is drought and dryness in the land, I will enjoy wetness and freshness in Jesus' name.
3. ***Deut 11:24;*** I take possession of this land in Jesus' name.
4. ***Deut 11:14;*** I receive the rains of this land in due season for a good harvest in Jesus' name.
5. ***Deut 11:15;*** I will eat in this land and be satisfied, in Jesus' name.
6. ***Deut 11:17;*** In Jesus' name, the heavens over me shall not be shut up against me in this land.

7. ***Matt 3:16;*** I shall operate under the open heavens in this land in Jesus' name.
8. ***Deut 11:25;*** Lord, no man or woman will be able to withstand me in this land, in Jesus' name.
9. ***Deut 11:26;*** I collect and gather all the blessings in this land in Jesus' name.
10. ***Isaiah 60:11; 45:2-3***; In Jesus' name, I command the gates into the treasures of this land to stay open for me to enter and possessing the blessings of this land.
11. ***Lev20:22;*** This land shall not vomit me out in Jesus' name.
12. ***Neh 9:36;*** I shall not become a slave to any situation or circumstance in this land, in Jesus' name.
13. ***Gen 26:13;*** Father, in this land I shall wax great, go forward, and grow until I become very great in Jesus' name.
14. ***Neh 8:7-8;*** Father, cause me to understand your word so I can take my place in this land in Jesus' name.
15. ***2 kings 19:30-31;*** I shall be established in this land in Jesus' name.
16. ***2 Sam 7:11;*** I receive rest in this land on every side in Jesus' name.
17. ***2 Sam 22:44;*** Wherever I find myself in this life, men and women will serve me with their substance;

- Wherever I find myself in this life, men and women will desire to support and be part of what I'm doing.
- In this life, wherever I find myself, men and women will desire to bless and favor me.

18. ***Rom 9:25-26;*** In this land where others have failed, I will succeed.

    - Where others have been rejected, I will be accepted.
    - Where others have been mocked and ridiculed, I shall be celebrated.

19. ***John 5:9; Ps 34:5;*** Whatever makes for shame and reproach in this land, roll it away from me in Jesus' name.
20. ***Isaiah 57:14;*** May every stumbling block in my way become a stepping stone in Jesus' name.

Ps 35:27; 3 John 2; Neh 2:20. When God saved you, what was in his mind concerning you was prosperity, and nothing short of that. Just as our success and victory make our earthly parents to rejoice, so is our prosperity makes God happy.

1. ***Gen 24:40;*** Father, wherever my prosperity, breakthrough, and blessing are tied down, I send your ministering angels to let them loose in Jesus' name.
2. ***Ps 23:1;34.10;*** I destroy the spirit of lack and want in my life by the Holy Ghost's fire in Jesus' name.
3. ***Gen 39:3;*** Father, from this day forth, I command that whatever I set my hands to do shall prosper exceedingly in Jesus' name.
4. ***Gen 39:23;*** Father, by the power of your word and the authority of the name of Jesus, make all that concern me to prosper in the matchless name of Jesus.

5. ***Josh: 1:7;1 kings 2:3;2*** Father, in the name of Jesus, wherever I go in this life, prosperity shall greet me in Jesus' name.
6. ***Job 29:6;*** Father, in Jesus' powerful name, I will dip my feet in butter, and the rock will pour out rivers of oil for me in this life.
7. ***Ps 1:3;*** Father, in the mighty name of Jesus, whatever I do in this life, whether big or small, I invoke the spirit of prosperity over it in Jesus' name.
8. ***Ps 122:6;*** Father, because I love your house, cause me to prosper in Jesus' name.
9. ***Ps 45:2-4;*** Father, I decree and command in the name of Jesus that every step I will take in life shall be prosperous in Jesus' name.
10. ***Dan 6:28;*** Father, I prophesy and declare that in every government regime, I shall experience prosperity and not be limited in Jesus' name.
11. ***1Sam 6-8;*** Father, connect me to men and women of prosperity in this life, in Jesus' name.
12. ***Job 36:11;*** Father, from this day forth, I shall spend my days and years in prosperity and pleasure, in Jesus' name.
13. ***Ps 118:25;*** Father, I beseech and ask that you send prosperity my way in Jesus' name.
14. ***Ps 112:3; Ps 112:3; 122:7-9;*** Father, in the name of Jesus, I command wealth, riches, and

prosperity upon my tabernacle in Jesus mighty name.

15. ***Gen 39:2;*** Father, as your presence made Joseph prosperous, so may you make me prosper in Jesus' name.
16. ***Josh 1:8;*** Father, in the name of Jesus, I decree and declare that you make all my ways prosper in Jesus' name.
17. ***Ps 35:27;*** Father, I prophesy that I will swim and wallow in prosperity all the days of my life, in Jesus' name.
18. Father, in the name of Jesus, I prophesy that each day of my life, as I wake up, prosperity shall be the first thing to greet me in Jesus' name.
19. Father, by the authority of your word and your name, I prophesy that prosperity shall be the trademark of my life in Jesus' name.
20. ***Eccl 11:6;*** Father, in the name of Jesus, anything short of prosperity in my life is terminated in the matchless name of Jesus.
21. ***2 Cor 8:9;*** Father, I ride on the wings of grace to the land of prosperity and riches in Jesus' name.
22. ***Deut 7:5;*** Any alter reacted against my prosperity, I smash and set them on fire in Jesus' name.
23. ***Phil 4:19;*** Father, from today forth, I will live in abundance and affluence and enjoy your full supply, in Jesus' name.

24. Heavenly Father, in the name of Jesus, wherever I find myself in this life, prosperity shall be the order of my day in Jesus' name.
25. ***Is 48:17;*** Father, in the name of Jesus, teach and guide me to the place of prosperity and profit in Jesus' name.
26. ***Ps 23:5;*** Prophesy, that in the midst of my adversaries and adversity, I will live in plenty in Jesus' name.
27. ***Ps 92:12;*** Where men/ women are finding it hard to survive and make it, I will flourish, like the palm tree, in Jesus' name.
28. ***Deut. 8:18;*** From today on, I receive divine empowerment to be prosperous and wealthy in Jesus' name.
29. ***Joel 2:6;*** From today I contact the power to live in plenty in Jesus' name.
30. ***Ps 34:10;*** Lord, in the name of Jesus, I will enjoy all-round and all-season prosperity in Jesus' name.
31. ***Jer 29:11;*** I prophesy, that the remaining days of my life shall be the best, blessed, and most prosperous days of my life in Jesus' name.

1. ***Deut 7:5;*** Lord any altar built against my life and destiny be consumed by Holy Ghost fire in Jesus' name.
2. ***Deut 7:10;*** Father, every spiritual philistine militating against my life, destiny, and everything that concerns me, I command thunder over them in Jesus' Christ name.
3. ***Ps 106:11;*** Lord, I release water to cover every one of my enemies in Jesus' name.
4. ***Ps 55:15;*** Father, whoever is against my life and destiny, let death overtake them in Jesus' name.
5. ***Ps 55:15;*** Father, wherever they meet to take counsel together against my life, Father, let them go down to hell quick in Jesus' name.
6. ***Num 16:31-33;*** Anyone who is against my progress and greatness, let the earth swallow them up in Jesus' name.
7. ***1 Sam 7:3;*** Father, I subdue every spiritual philistine that is against my life in Jesus' name.
8. ***Ps 105:24;*** Lord, make me stronger than all my enemies in Jesus' name.
9. ***Gen 19:24;*** Any man/ woman who says it will not be well with me, I rain down coals of fire and brimstone upon them in Jesus' name.

10. ***Ps 55:23;*** Anyone who says I will not live the full number of my days, bring them down into their destruction in Jesus' name.
11. ***Ps 55:19;*** Lord, any agent of Satan that is sent to resist and to oppose my life, my future, and my destiny, I afflict them with............. (Mention what you want God to afflict them with.)
12. ***Gen 12:3;*** Anybody that has ever opened his/her mouth to curse and to say all manner of evil against me, I multiply it a thousand times and send it back to sender in Jesus' name.
13. ***Ps 109:6;*** Anyone who says that it will not be better with my life, family, business, and office should set a wicked man over him, and may Satan stand by him and condemn him in Jesus' name.
14. ***Ps 109:8;*** Whoever it is that is fighting against my life, well-being, and progress in my office, let his days be few and let another take his office.
15. ***Ps 109:17-18;*** Whoever cursed me and spoke evil of my life, future, and destiny, I return it back to them 100-fold in Jesus Christ name.
16. ***Ps 124:7;*** Wherever my blessings and breakthroughs have been caged, I break out and escape in Jesus' name.
17. ***Num 23:11;*** Whoever that has cursed me, I turn it into blessings in Jesus' name.

18. ***Ps 109:29;*** All my enemies that are looking for my downfall, I cover them with shame and set them in confusion in Jesus' name.
19. ***Ps 110:1-2;*** Lord all my enemies, I put them under my feet and rule over them in Jesus' name.
20. ***Jer 16:16;*** Wherever they are hiding and scheming evil against me, I release the fishers and hunters to fish them out in Jesus' name.
21. ***Jer 30:23;*** Lord, let your whirlwind carry away every one of my enemies in Jesus' name.
22. ***Ps 18:14;*** I release spiritual arrows and bullets to locate my enemies wherever they are hiding and shoot them in Jesus' name.
23. ***Joel 2:25; 1 Sam 7:14;*** Whatever the enemy has taken or stolen from me, be restored in Jesus' name.
24. ***2 Sam 15:31;*** I turn all the counsel of the enemies against my life into foolishness in Jesus' name.
25. ***Ex 14:27–28;*** Any man/ woman that is against me, my family, or my business, let the Sea swallow them in Jesus' name.
26. ***2 Sam 22:15;*** Lord, wherever evil conspirators are gathered and are conspiring against my life in this land, let your arrows scatter them in Jesus' name.

27. ***Job 5:12;*** Father, disappoint all the devices of the crafty over my life; their hands will never carry out their enterprise over my life in Jesus' name.
28. ***Hos 9:14;*** Wherever the Satanic apostles have been stationed to scheme and strategize against me, give them a miscarrying womb in Jesus' name.
29. ***Isaiah 28:6;*** Every satanic gate that is open against me be broken and consumed by the Holy Ghost fire.
30. ***Isaiah 54:14;*** I frustrate every weapon the enemy has fashioned against me in Jesus' name.
31. ***Isaiah 57:20;*** Any man/ woman learning wickedness against me, I trouble them with everlasting trouble and declare they will never have rest in life, in Jesus' name.
32. ***Psalms 55:23;*** Every wicked and evil man that stands in my way of progress and lifting, bring them down into the pit of destruction. Let them not live half their days in Jesus' name.
33. ***Ps 35:4;*** Whoever is looking for my downfall anywhere in this life, let them be put to shame and be confounded in Jesus' name.
34. ***Ps 35:5-6;*** Wherever they gather to scheme for my destruction, I release the Angels of God to chase and persecute them in Jesus' name.
35. ***Ps 35:8;*** Whatever net and trap they have set against me, let it catch them in Jesus' name.

36. ***Ex 14:26-28;*** Every spiritual evil pursuing my life, I command the sea to swallow them in Jesus' name.
37. ***Isaiah 54:17;*** Where the enemies have gathered to condemn my life, I condemn them in the matchless name of Jesus.
38. ***Isaiah 61:7;*** Every garment of shame and reproach in my life, I remove and set it on fire, in Jesus' name.
39. ***Ps 68:1-2;*** Oh Lord, arise, and let all your enemies be scattered in the name of Jesus.
40. ***Ex 4:9;*** Father, in the name of Jesus, I pronounce the death sentence over any man/ woman trying to eliminate my life in the mighty name of Jesus.

Prov 18:2; Eccl 4:9; Heb 13:4; Marriage is the will of God, and God's heart is in it. It is not only for better and for worse, but it is also for a better living. It is to better the lives of those in it and bring them honor.

1. ***Deut 7:5;*** Every satanic alter that rises against my family and marriage, Holy Ghost fire consume it in Jesus' name.
2. ***gen 3:12;*** Lord, unite me and my spouse with a strong cord of love in Jesus' name.
3. ***Prov 3:13;*** Every spirit sent from the pit of hell to cause confusion, quarrels, fights, and a lack of peace and harmony in my family and marriage be destroyed by the Holy Ghost's fire in Jesus' name.
4. Every manipulating spirit and all evil activities in my marriage are destroyed by the blood of Jesus.
5. ***Num 23:23;*** Let every evil manipulation and manifestation in my home and marriage be consumed and destroyed by the Holy Ghost's fire.
6. ***Duet 7:14;*** I destroy all forms of barrenness in my home and marriage, be they financial, spiritual, physical, etc., in Jesus' name.

7. ***Ex 23:26;*** Every delay in conception in my marriage comes to an end in Jesus' name.
8. ***Ps 91:13;*** Every arrow released by the enemy to attack my family and marriage, whether in the daytime or nighttime, is sent back to the sender in Jesus' name.
9. ***Ps 91:13;*** Every lion, serpent, and cobra sent to attack and disintegrate my family and marriage, I trample them under my feet in Jesus' name.
10. ***Num 23:23;*** Wherever our pictures (me and my spouse) have been taken for evil, holy ghost fire thunder over them in Jesus' name.
11. ***Josh 5:9;*** Whatever curses, shame and reproach towards my home and marriage, will never succeed against my home and marriage in Jesus' name.
12. ***Isaiah 25:8;*** Every spirit of death hovering around my home, marriage, and spouse should be swallowed up in victory in Jesus' name.
13. ***Isaiah 65:23;*** My children shall be a blessing and not a problem or curse, in Jesus' name.
14. ***Ps 44:21;*** Every secret plan of the wicked against my children in all their ways is disorganized and destroyed in the name of Jesus.
15. Every monitoring gadget and torch light monitoring my family, home, and marriage is set ablaze by the Holy Ghost's fire in Jesus' name.

16. Ha*g 1:6;* Whatever spirit sent to steal our money and blessings, is set in perpetual confusion in Jesus' name.
17. ***Eph 6:12;*** I disarm and dethrone all satanic Kings, rulers, authorities, powers, and spiritual wickedness against my home, family, and marriage in Jesus' name.
18. All satanic agents sent to snatch my husband/ wife be disorganized and destroyed in Jesus' name.
19. ***Mal 2:16;*** All the plans and strategies of the enemy mapped out to destroy and disintegrate my marriage, and the spirits sent to execute those plans, are destroyed by the blood of Jesus.
20. Whatever the devil is using as a point of contact to afflict my marriage and home is set ablaze by the Holy Ghost's fire.
21. ***Heb 13:4;*** Father, restore the honor and dignity of my home and marriage in Jesus' name.
22. ***Ps 1:3;*** As a family and as a couple, whatever we lay our hands on, to do shall prosper in Jesus' name.
23. ***Prov 18:22;*** I set in motion the favor that is meant for my home and marriage in Jesus' name.

Num 23:23: There are a lot of negative things that happen to us which are as a result of evil manifestation and manipulation. Here are our scriptural bullets and arrows to deal with and subdue all evil manipulation and manifestation in your life.

1. Every evil eye watching and casting bad spells for me in my finances, family, business, and office is destroyed by the blood of Jesus.
2. ***Rev 12:10; Zech 3:1-2***; Every accusing voice speaking against me in my place of work and business, against my success, blessings, and breakthroughs, I silence them by the blood of Jesus.
3. Every evil sent to fight against my blessings and prosperity, to make me poor and wretched, is destroyed them by the blood of Jesus Christ.
4. Any charm or any object dropped in my office to militate against me and to oppose me in all my ways and families are destroyed by the blood of Jesus and Holy Ghost fire.

5. ***Jer 16:16-17;*** I release the angels of God to search and subdue all forces and satanic apostles stationed in strategic areas of my life to stop the blessing of God coming my way, in Jesus' name.
6. ***Deut 20:4;*** Every curse and its effects that have been humiliating my life and family from the third and fourth generations behind me, I destroy and disconnect myself from them in the matchless name of Jesus.
7. All powers of evil sent from my relatives, either from the maternal or paternal side, are destroyed by the holy name of Jesus.
8. ***2 Chr 20:22–23;*** All the warring spirits and forces sent to attack, resist, and oppose me, and hinder family progress and success, I send them in perpetual confusion in Jesus' name.
9. ***Hag 1:5-6;*** All the satanic spirits sent to siphon my money and blessings are destroyed by the Holy Ghost's fire.
10. ***1 Sam 7:10;*** Whatever the devil is using as a point of contact to attack my life, finances, and family, I thunder them with the Holy Ghost thunder in Jesus' name.
11. ***Ps 18:45;*** Every bad odor or smell the devil has inflicted on me that drives away the blessings, favor, and men and women that God sent to be a blessing to me is destroyed in Jesus' name.

12. ***Rom 13:14;*** I clothe myself, my family, and my business with the smell of God in Jesus' name.
13. ***Isaiah 8:10;*** Every evil arrangement from East to West, from North to South against me, my family, and my businesses in my office will be scattered by the blood of Jesus.
14. Every evil initiation, whether in dreams or through food, or by any other means, I revoke and disconnect myself from it in Jesus' name.
15. I disorganize whatever they have organized, and I disconnect all their connections against me in Jesus' name.
16. ***Ps 45:5;*** Any evil standing in my way of progress and greatness, I release spiritual arrows to locate and shoot them in Jesus' name.
17. ***Num 23:23;*** Wherever my picture/ image, or name has been taken for enchantment and divination, I release the Holy Ghost thunder to thunder them in Jesus' name.
18. All forms of demonic activities in my life and business be consumed by the Holy Ghost's fire.
19. I cancel every evil verdict against my life in Jesus' name.
20. I cancel and frustrate any magical power set in motion to fight me in Jesus' name

Ps 121:4–8; Ps 127:1–4; Jehovah God has promised and is committed to keeping and preserving us from all the wickedness of the wicked.

1. ***Ps 91:5;*** Every arrow of the enemy targeted at me in the daytime or at nighttime shall never succeed over me, I take refuge in God in Jesus' name.
2. ***Is 34:5-6;*** Father I claim my deliverance from all afflictions of life in Jesus' name.
3. ***Ps 4:5;*** Father, in all my ways, surround me with your fire, and let your glory defend me in Jesus' name.
4. Father, in the midst of difficulties and hardship, shield me in Jesus' name.
5. ***Prov 18:10;*** Father, for every evil that is connected to the sun, moon, and stars against me, I take refuge in you in Jesus' name.
6. ***Ps 121:7;*** Father, preserve my life, family, and business from all forms of evil in Jesus' name.
7. ***Ps 121:8;*** Father, whether in the daytime or nighttime, preserve my life in Jesus' name.

8. I set all the satanic apostles and all the agents Satan uses against me, I set them in perpetual confusion in Jesus' name.
9. ***Ps 91:11 I;*** release the Guardian angels sent to take care of me into operation in Jesus' name.
10. Every trap and pit the enemy has set before me, let them fall inside in Jesus' name.
11. ***Ex 13:21;*** Father, I release a pillar of cloud to cover and protect me by day and a pillar of fire to go before me by night and in all my ways, in Jesus' name.
12. ***Ps 91:13;*** Father, shield me from the lions and serpents of life that will rise against me in Jesus' name.
13. ***Ps 91:3;*** Every fowler's snare set against me and my family, office, and business place, I escape in Jesus' name.
14. Father, I declare that in the midst of turbulence and insecurity, I shall be secure in the name of Jesus.
15. ***Ps 34:7;*** May the angel you have sent my way constantly surround me and preserve me from all harm, in Jesus' name.
16. ***2 Chr. 20:22;*** Father, in the triumphant name of Jesus, I will confuse any ambush laid against me by my enemies.

17. ***Prov 18:10;*** Holy Father, in the midst of calamity and disaster, I take refuge in your name, in Jesus' name.
18. ***Ps 23:4;*** Father, in the midst of a hostile and dangerous environment, I clothe myself with your presence in Jesus' name.
19. ***Ps 62:2–3;*** Father, as I get through life, keep and hide me beyond the reach of my enemies in Jesus' name.
20. ***Job 5:21;*** Father, protect me from every scourging tongue in this life, in Jesus' name

Ps 102:13; We live in a crooked, perverted and sinful world where life is hard. You need the favor of God more than ever. The arrival of favor in your life results in the termination of emptiness, poverty, lack, and want in your life. Now is the set time for favors to be set in motion in your life.

1. ***Est 2:15;*** Father, like Esther in a foreign land, I shall obtain favor before kings and princesses, and I shall be preferred above others in this life in Jesus' name.
2. ***Deut 33:23;*** Father, I invoke your favor upon me to bring satisfaction and all-round blessings to my life in Jesus' name.
3. ***Ex 3:21;*** Father, grant me favor in the midst of my enemies, in Jesus' name.
4. I command every emptiness, bareness, lack, and want in my life to be terminated by the force of favor upon me in Jesus' name.
5. ***Rom 9:29-33;*** Wherever men and women have been rejected, molested, humiliated, mocked, and

disfavored in this life, I shall be accepted and highly favored in Jesus' name.

6. ***Ps 5:12;*** Father, compass me all round with favor as with a shield, in Jesus' name.
7. ***Prov 18:22;*** Father, for the favor that is for my home and marriage, I set it in motion right now in Jesus' name.
8. ***Esth 2:15;*** Father, grant me favor before men and women of substance, influence, and affluence, in Jesus' name.
9. ***Acts 2:47;*** Father, I decree and declare that wherever I find myself, men and women will desire to help me in Jesus' name.
10. ***Dan 1:9;*** Father, in the office, business place, etc., grant me favor with my boss.
11. ***Prov 22:1-2,22-23;*** Father, favor me and cause me to sit, dine, and interact with kings in this life, in Jesus' name.
12. Father, in this life I will matter where it matters because of your favor toward me, in Jesus' name.
13. ***Luke 2:52;*** Father, grant me your favor so that everywhere I enter, no man or woman will resist or oppose me, in Jesus' name.
14. ***1 Kings 11:23;*** Father, in the name of Jesus, I receive open doors and breakthroughs that I am not qualified for in Jesus' name.
15. ***Prov 19:12;*** As the dew falls upon the grass, let your favor come up for me in Jesus' name.

16. ***Ps 30:7;*** Father, by your favor, I shall be strong financially, materially, and in all areas of my life, in Jesus' name.
17. Father, I receive divine favor in every ramification of my life, in Jesus' name.
18. ***Ex 12:13;*** Father, in the name of Jesus, grant me such a favor that everywhere I find myself in this life, none of my requests shall be turned down in Jesus' name.

1. Favor is God showing you kind regard. ***Ex 3:21***
2. Favor is having popularity with God. ***Gen 18:17-18***
3. Favor is God giving you approval. ***Matt 3:17***
4. Favor is God treating you with care.
5. Favor is God showing you a special preference. ***Esth 2:17***
6. Favor is God's way of partnering with you.
7. Favor is God's way of giving you special attention.

IS 54:2; Jer 29:6-7;

1. ***Is 54:3-4;*** Father, I break any limitations and restrictions placed against me in Jesus' name.
2. ***Ps 115:14;*** Father, in the name of Jesus, I command an increase in my finances, business, and whatever I lay my hands on to do in Jesus' name.
3. ***Ex 1:12;*** Father, in the midst of adversity, I will advance, In the midst of frustration, I will be fruitful, In the midst of affliction, I shall live in affluence, in Jesus' name.
4. ***Job 8:7;*** Father, in this life I will never be small, but a great man/ woman in Jesus' name.
5. ***Ps 71:20-21;*** Father, in the name of Jesus, I shall experience increase on every side of my life in Jesus' name.
6. ***Deut 28:13;*** Father, wherever I find myself in this life, I will always be on top and not beneath, in Jesus' name.
7. Father, in my life, family, business, or working place in this land and in society at large, enlarge and increase me to be beckoned to be reckoned with in Jesus' name.
8. ***Is 54:2;*** I refuse to remain in the same spot (stagnation). I am moving forward, and I will

experience progress in every area of my life, in Jesus’ name.

9. ***Gen 26:13;*** Father, in this life I will work great, go forward, and increase until I become very great in Jesus’ name.
10. ***Ps 106:24;*** Father, whoever is competing with me, increase me in every area above them, in Jesus' name.
11. ***Jer 29:6;*** Father, I will live a life of increase and not diminishment, in Jesus' name.
12. ***Ps 65:5-13;*** Father, in this life the earth shall produce and yield her increase for me in Jesus' name.

Gal 3:13-14; If there is an enemy that is fighting the human race tooth and nail, it is the enemy called poverty. It has no mercy in its blood. That is why you need to fight it without fear, fight it without mercy, fight it without looking back, fight it with every bit of your strength, and fight it with passion. Remember, Jesus has paid the price for you to be free from the bondage of poverty, but He is still hovering around you. Here are some spiritual bullets and arrows to break and destroy the backbone of poverty permanently in your life.

1. I curse and smite the spirit of poverty out of my life in Jesus' name.
2. Father, in the name of Jesus, I erase my name from the Register of Poverty by the blood of Jesus.
3. ***Is 10:27;*** the yoke and grip of poverty over my life, I destroy it by the Holy Ghost's fire in Jesus' name.

4. ***Deut 15:4;*** Father, the spirit of poverty hovering in my home and among my family members is destroyed in Jesus' name.
5. ***1 Sam 2:8;*** Father, in the name of Jesus from today I walk out on poverty in the name of Jesus.
6. ***Ps 113:7;*** Father, in the name of Jesus, by the power of your redemptive work, I begin to operate above and beyond the realm of poverty in Jesus' name.
7. "Father, in the name of Jesus, instead of allowing poverty to destroy me, I destroy it in my life in His name," says ***Proverbs 10:15.***
8. ***Deut 7:5;*** Father, every altar erected to keep me poor and every covenant or agreement signed on my behalf, knowingly or unknowingly, are destroyed and revoked by the fire of the Holy Ghost in Jesus' name.
9. ***Heb 12:24-29;*** You spirit of poverty and lack, the blood of Jesus is against you in my life, in Jesus' name.
10. Father, in the name of Jesus, in my family line, I disconnect myself from the spirit of poverty that is operating there in Jesus' name.
11. ***Matt 15:13;*** By the authority of the word of God, I uproot poverty from its roots in my life, in Jesus' name.
12. ***Deut 33:27;*** Lord, from today on, I will unseat and dethrone every satanic strongman and

stronghold stationed against me to keep me poor, in Jesus' name.

13. ***Job 5:22;*** I decree and declare that in the midst of lack, want, and hardship, I will laugh in Jesus' name.

Isaiah 53:5, 3; 1John 2; Ex 15:20-26; and 15:26; It is God's desire for his children to enjoy healing and divine health. No matter what Satan tells you, please know that your healing was perfected in the Redemption. Gal 3:13-14.

1. I release and disconnect myself from any sickness or disease I inherited from my parents and grandparents, in Jesus' name.
2. ***Ps 18:45-46;*** I command every stranger or hidden sickness or disease in my life to die in the mighty name of Jesus.
3. I destroy every satanic dropping in every department of my body. Holy Ghost fire consume them in Jesus' name.
4. ***Ps 18:14;*** Every arrow of infirmity released to attack my health; I send it back to the sender in Jesus' name.
5. ***Gal 3:13-14;*** Father, in the name of Jesus, I claim my healing and redemption in His name.
6. ***1 John 4:4;*** I declare my victory over every form of sickness and disease in my life in Jesus' name.

7. ***Isaiah 49:25;*** Any sickness or disease that contends with me, Father, fight it in Jesus' name.
8. ***Isaiah 49:18-23;*** Whatever fights the soldiers of my body and the antibodies that help to resist sickness and disease in my body, go away from me now in Jesus' name.
9. ***Isaiah 54:17;*** Any germ, virus, or bacteria that causes sickness or disease, I command you to die whenever you touch my body in Jesus' name.
10. Any blood-related sickness or disease I command the blood of Jesus to neutralize its power and effect in my blood, in Jesus' name.
11. Lord Jesus, transfuse me with your blood in Jesus' name.
12. I command every germ, parasite, and poison working against my health to be neutralized by the fire of the Holy Spirit in Jesus name.
13. I command every part of my body that is out of order to be back in order now, in Jesus' name.
14. I destroy the yoke of seasonal or periodical sickness and disease in my life in the matchless name of Jesus.
15. ***Ps 18:45;*** I command every agent of sickness and disease in my blood and body organs to die and fade away in Jesus' name.
16. ***Ps 18:45;*** I command my blood and body to reject any foreign entity in Jesus' name.

17. ***Heb 12:24;*** Every form of infirmity that humiliates and mocks my life, let the blood of Jesus speak disappearance to it now, in Jesus' name.
18. ***Isaiah 25:8;*** I disarm all forms of engagement and appointment with the spirit of death in Jesus' name.
19. I command all forms of parasites that make strange movements in my body at specific times of the day or night to die by the blood of Jesus.
20. All the hidings, refuges, and abodes of sickness and disease in my body, I command you not to accommodate them in Jesus' name.
21. ***John 10:10;*** I command every dead organ in my body to receive life now in Jesus' name.
22. Father, in the name of Jesus, let the blood of Jesus flush out every evil deposit from my blood.
23. Any evil foreign entity, germ, bacteria, or virus that touches my body, I command my body and blood to reject them in the name of Jesus.
24. ***Zech 9:11;*** I hold the blood of Jesus against my spirit because... (mention what is disturbing you) in the name of Jesus.
25. ***Isaiah 49:24-25;*** I destabilize and destroy every legal ground that the enemy is using to afflict my life with sickness and disease, in Jesus' name.
26. I engage the forces of heaven, the forces of nature, and the blood of the resurrected Christ to

resist, oppose, frustrate, attack, and challenge every sickness or disease militating against me in Jesus' name.

27. ***Lk 13:12;*** With the authority of the word of God and the power of the name of Jesus, I free myself from every infirmity in His name.
28. ***Ex 23:25;*** In Jesus' name, I command you to expel all sickness and disease from my life.

2 Tim 1:7; Fear and intimidation are weapons the devil uses to rob us of what is rightfully ours. Fear is a robber of destiny; it takes the destined winner, captive. Fear is not of God but of the devil, for it has torment. 1 John 4:18; Fear makes you say and see things that are not real. Numb 13:27-33; (The ten spies saw the giants, and fear gripped them.) The greatest liars of a man are his fears, e.g., the lepers in 2 kings. 7:3-10

10. Sometimes fear makes people run from safety to danger. Fear is a tyrant, but through the power of the name of Jesus, you will not be tyrannized by this monster called fear in His name. Job 3: 25 Fear has a force that attracts evil to its victim. God said to have no fear because Jesus lives. You can face tomorrow with confidence in Jesus' name.

1. ***Jdgs 6:23;*** I bind you with the foul spirit of fear that makes me fear death in Jesus' name.
2. ***Ps 23:4;*** I take authority over the fear of evil in my life in the powerful name of Jesus.
3. From now on, I will intimidate every spirit of intimidation in my life, in Jesus' name.
4. ***Ps 31:13***; From whatever angle and area the enemy may try to attack me with fear, I turn it away in Jesus' name.
5. ***Ps 119:39;*** Father, whatever situation or circumstance that makes me fearful, I ask that you turn it away from me in Jesus' name.
6. ***Is 8:12;*** Whatever terrorizes men and women and makes them fear greatly, I refuse to be intimidated by it in Jesus' name.
7. ***Is 43:12;*** My father, in Jesus' name, let your presence neutralize every form of fear in and around me.
8. ***Is 54:4;*** I shame, disgrace every disgrace, and disappoint every disappointment in my life in Jesus' name.
9. ***Ps 91:5;*** I overcome every terrorizing spirit against me both during the day and at night, in Jesus' name

1. ***Gen 22:17;*** Father, in the name of Jesus, my life shall be the epitome and embodiment of your blessings, in Jesus' name.
2. ***Gen 26:3;*** So, other than your presence, which attracted blessings upon the life of Isaac, may your presence attract your blessings upon me, in Jesus' name.
3. In the name of Jesus, your blessings upon me shall be evident in every aspect of my life, in Jesus' name.
4. ***Deut 23:20; Neh 13:2;*** Any man/ woman that has ever opened his or her mouth to curse me, turn it into blessings in Jesus' name.
5. ***Numb 24:1;*** Father, be pleased with me and bless me in Jesus' name.
6. In the name of Jesus, may your blessings increase and multiply in my life.
7. In the name of Jesus, bless me greatly beyond measure.
8. ***Deut 15: 10;*** I command your blessings upon all that I set my hands to do, and the work of my hands shall prosper greatly in Jesus' name.
9. ***1 Chr 4:10;*** Father, I don't just want you to bless me, but to bless me indeed in Jesus' name.

10. ***Psalm 5:12;*** Father, bless me in Jesus' name because I am the righteousness of God in Christ Jesus.
11. ***Ps 115:12-13;*** Father, I command your blessing upon all my family members, both small and great, in Jesus' name.
12. ***Deut 28:3;*** Father, prophesy your blessing upon me in the city and out of the city in Jesus' name.
13. ***Deut. 28:4–5;*** Father, I declare your blessing upon whatever is mine in Jesus' name.
14. ***Deut 28:6;*** I decree your blessing upon my coming in and going out in Jesus' name.
15. ***Deut 28:8;*** Father, I release your blessings upon my bank account and in all that I do, and I process your blessing in this land in Jesus' name.
16. ***Deut 28:12;*** I command the heavens to be open for me, and from this day forth I will begin to operate under an open heaven, in Jesus' name.
17. ***Gen 26:13;*** I decree that your blessing will cause me to wax great, go forward, and grow until I become very great in Jesus' name.
18. ***2 Sam 6:11;*** As the Ark of the Covenant, attracted your blessing, so may your presence attract your blessings upon my household, in Jesus' name.
19. ***Gen 12:2;*** says, Father, bless me abundantly so I can be a channel of blessing to others in Jesus' name."

20. ***Gen. 27: 35–36;*** Father, wherever my blessings are, no man or woman will take them away in Jesus' name.
21. ***Lev 25:21;*** Father, in the name of Jesus, I command your blessings upon me, my business office, and my family members, in Jesus' name.
22. ***Ps 109:17;*** Anyone who does not want me to be blessed, may blessings be far away from him in Jesus' name.
23. ***Ezk 34:26;*** Father, shower my life with showers of blessing in Jesus' name.
24. ***Ezk 47:5;*** Father, in the name of Jesus, may you bless me with an oversized blessing in your name.

I have given, and it is given unto me in good measure, pressed down, shaken together, running over, men given unto my bosom. ***Luke 6:38.***

****

With what measure I meet, it is measured unto me. I sow bountifully; therefore, I reap bountifully. I give cheerfully, and my God has made all grace abound toward me, and I, having all sufficiency of all things, do abound in all good works. ***II Corinthians 9:6–8.***

****

There is no lack for my God, who supplies all of my needs according to His riches in glory in Christ Jesus. ***Philippians 4:19.***

****

The Lord is my shepherd, and I do not want because Jesus was made poor so that I might, through his poverty, have abundance, for he came that I might have life and have it more abundantly. ***Psalms 23:1; II Corinthians 8:9; John 10:10.***

****

And I, having received the gift of righteousness, do resign as a king in the life of Jesus Christ. ***Romans 5:17.***

For wisdom and guidance, confess these three times a day;

The Spirit of Truth abides in me and teaches me all things, and he guides me into all truth. Therefore, I confess that I have perfect knowledge of every situation and every circumstance that I come up against. for I have the wisdom of God. ***John 16:13; James 1:5.***

****

I trust in the Lord with all my heart, and I lean not toward my own understanding. ***Proverbs 3:5.***

****

In all my ways, I acknowledge him, and he directs my path. ***Proverbs 3:6.***

****

The word of God is a lamp unto my feet; it is a light unto my path. ***Psalms 119:105.***

****

The Lord will perfect what concerns me. ***Psalms 138:8.***

****

I let the word of Christ dwell richly in me in all wisdom. ***Colossians 3:16.***

****

I do follow the good shepherd, and I know his voice; the voice of a stranger I will not follow. ***John 10: 4-5.***

www.ingramcontent.com/pod-product-compliance
Lightning Source LLC
LaVergne TN
LVHW050343160826
845677LV00014B/3764